SNOW MONKEYS

MONKEY DISCOVERY LIBRARY

Lynn M. Stone

Rourke Corporation, Inc.
Vero Beach, Florida 32964

PHOTO CREDITS

All photos © Lynn M. Stone

ACKNOWLEDGEMENTS

The author thanks the following for photographic assistance:
The Milwaukee County Zoo, Milwaukee, Wis.

LIBRARY OF CONGRESS
Library of Congress Cataloging-in-Publication Data
Stone, Lynn M.
  Snow Monkeys / by Lynn M. Stone.

  p. cm. — (Monkey discovery library)
  Summary: Describes the habitat, lifestyle, infancy, predators,
relationship with humans, and future of this intelligent primate.
  ISBN 0-86593-066-X
  1. Japanese macaqua—Juvenile literature. [1. Japanese
macaqua. 2. Monkeys.] I. Title. II. Series: Stone, Lynn M.
Monkey discovery library.
QL737.P93S763 1990
599.8'24—dc20   90-31940
                                 CIP
                                 AC

Snow Monkey

TABLE OF CONTENTS

The Snow Monkey   5
The Snow Monkey's Cousins   6
How They Look   9
Where They Live   11
How They Live   14
The Snow Monkey's Babies   16
Predator and Prey   19
The Snow Monkey and People   20
The Snow Monkey's Future   22
Glossary   23
Index   24

THE SNOW MONKEY

The snow monkey *(Macaca fuscata)* is the Santa Claus of the money kingdom. Like St. Nick, it has a pink face, beard, and bright eyes, and it lives in a cold climate.

Most monkeys live in warm places. The snow monkey, or Japanese macaque (pronounced mah-CACK), lives in a **habitat,** or home, which is very unusual for a monkey.

Snow falls in the mountains where the macaque lives. No wonder that the Japanese macaque is often called snow monkey.

THE SNOW MONKEY'S COUSINS

Snow monkeys are closely related to other monkeys and apes.

These animals, along with people, are the higher **primates.** Most primates have large brains and rather flat faces. Their hands and feet can grasp objects.

The snow monkey's closest cousins are 18 other **species,** or kinds, of macaques.

All macaques live either in Asia or northwest Africa.

The crab-eating macaque, rhesus monkey, and Taiwanese macaque are the monkeys most like the snow monkey.

Long-tailed Macaque baby

HOW THEY LOOK

Snow monkeys are well-dressed for life in cold weather. The pink face of a snow monkey peers out from under a hood of fur.

In winter, snow monkeys' fur is long and shaggy. They have less fur during the warm months.

Snow monkey fur can be brownish or nearly white.

Like other macaques, Japanese macaques are medium-sized monkeys. They have stocky legs, fairly heavy bodies, and short tails.

*Snow Monkey
with baby*

WHERE THEY LIVE

Snow monkeys live in Japan on the northern islands of Honshu, Shikoku, Kyushu, and Yakushima.

The snow monkey's habitat is the mountain forests of these islands.

In one of the mountain parks, snow monkeys have learned how to warm up on cold days. The monkeys bathe in hot springs.

Even in winter, the spring water is 104 degrees.

Snow Monkey

Snow Monkey removing snow

HOW THEY LIVE

Snow monkeys live in groups called **troops.** A troop may have over 500 monkeys.

Snow monkeys are fine climbers, but they usually travel and feed on the ground.

A snow monkey spends much of the day searching for food.

Like other monkeys, snow monkeys also take time for play and **grooming.** Grooming is the cleaning and combing of fur. Using their fingers, the monkeys clean out dirt, dead skin, and insects.

Snow monkeys huddle together for warmth and sleep in trees.

*Snow Monkey
grooming baby*

THE SNOW MONKEY'S BABIES

A snow monkey is born in the spring. During its first few months, it lives on its mother's milk. It travels with its mother by clinging to her belly.

The mother has another baby a year later. The older youngster walks along with its mother or rides on her back.

By age three to five, a snow monkey is ready to have its own family.

Snow monkeys in captivity have lived over 25 years.

*Snow Monkey
with Baby*

PREDATOR AND PREY

Snow monkeys are rarely hunters, or **predators.** They eat only a few little animals, insects, and eggs. Animals that the monkeys do catch are their **prey.**

Most of a snow monkey's diet is made up of plants. Snow monkeys eat berries, grain, fruit, seeds, flowers, tree bark, buds, and leaves.

In a park near Nagano, Japan, park rangers feed snow monkeys barley, apples, and soybeans.

Snow Monkeys feeding

THE SNOW MONKEY AND PEOPLE

Japanese people enjoy their snow monkeys. The monkey is one of Japan's most loved wild animals.

At the park near Nagano, snow monkeys mix with human visitors. The monkeys there have become tame because of the food they are given by rangers.

The group of macaque monkeys has always had close ties to people. Macaques are used in studies by scientists. They have been trained for circuses and for picking coconuts.

Macaques are hunted for food in some countries.

THE SNOW MONKEY'S FUTURE

Snow monkeys are carefully protected by the Japanese. Still, the number of snow monkeys has been dropping since the 1920's.

The problem for snow monkeys is the loss of their home—their habitat. Although the monkeys are protected, not all of their habitat is.

Japan is a small country with a large human population. Wood is needed, but when the mountain forests are cut, the troops of monkeys disappear.

Japan will be able to save its snow monkeys as long as it saves the monkeys' forests.

Glossary

grooming (GROO ming)—using the fingers to comb and clean fur

habitat (HAB a tat)—the kind of place in which an animal lives, such as a forest

predator (PRED a tor)—an animal that kills other animals for food

prey (PRAY)—an animal that is hunted by another for food

primate (PRI mate)—the group of mammals which includes monkeys, apes, and man

species (SPEE sheez)—within a group of closely related animals, one certain kind

troop (TROOP)—a group of monkeys or apes

INDEX

age 16
babies 16
beard 5
color 6
face 5, 6
food 19
fur 9, 14

grooming 14
habitat 5, 14, 22
Japan 14, 20, 22
macaques 6, 20
prey 19
primates 6
tail 6
troop 14